Christ's *Kids* Create!

VOLUME 1
Favorite Craft Ideas

Deborah Stroh & Vicki Boston

Dear Teacher:

This book exists to give you, the teacher, ideas to help reinforce the Christian concepts and themes you teach during religion class and integrate through all subjects.

With an emphasis on what is most manageable for the busy teacher, these projects are quick, easy, and inviting while still offering creative and keepable results. In many instances, specific suggestions for materials and sizes are not given. This is because some children need a starting point and directions to follow while others need only the

starting point. Therefore, the goal of this book is to lau[nch] you toward supplementary activities and crafts that help you communicate the Gospel message and encou[rage] students to learn as they experiment and create. To [this] end, each project offered here teaches Bible storie[s or] concepts. In some instances, the project has a clea[r] specific connection. But many of them are intenti[onally] generic so you can adapt them to reinforce a var[iety of] stories, concepts, or themes.

CONCORDIA PUBLISHING HOUSE · SAINT LOUIS

Written by Debbie Stroh and Vicki Boston
Illustrated by Debbie Stroh

Scripture quotations marked NIV are taken from the Holy Bible, New International Version®. NIV®. Copyright © 1973, 1978, 1984 by International Bible Society. Used by permission of Zondervan Publishing House. All rights reserved.

Scripture quotations marked KJV are from the King James or Authorized Version of the Bible.

This publication may be available in braille, in large print, or on cassette tape for the visually impaired. Please allow 8 to 12 weeks for delivery. Write to the Library for the Blind, 7550 Watson Rd., St. Louis, MO 63119-4409; call 1-866-215-6852; or e-mail to blind.mission@blindmission.org.

Manufactured in the United States of America

1 2 3 4 5 6 7 8 9   14 13 12 11 10 09 08 07 06

CONTENTS

Printed Banner   6

Banners are a great way to help children remember Bible stories, learn verses for memory work, and share their faith in the Triune God. Suggested Bible stories for this banner project are: creation, Noah's ark, Pentecost.

Window Shade Banner   7

A creative way to celebrate God's gifts, this window shade banner offers limitless imaginative outlet. Suggested Bible stories: Christmas, gifts from God, Jesus blesses the children.

Scripture Alphabet Banner   8

This project encourages Bible literacy, as it requires that children search for verses that begin with each letter of the alphabet. For example, Genesis 1:30, Matthew 5:7, 1 Chronicles 9:21.

Witness Rocks   16

Lead students on a hike or nature walk and have them look for smooth stones. Small stones can be kept in pockets as prayer rocks. Larger stones can be used as paperweights or gifts. Suggested verses and concepts: Psalm 18:2, Psalm 118:24, Psalm 61:2, Matthew 16:18, the parable of the wise man and the foolish man.

Sandcasting   17

Best for simple shapes, this activity will be a classroom favorite. Suggested Bible stories: Good Friday, Easter, fishers of men, coin in the fish's mouth, Jesus feeds 5,000, etc.

Noah's Ark   24

Ideal for young students, this activity is especially appealing to teachers because it uses inexpensive, readily available materials. Suggested Bible stories: Noah's ark, Jonah and the big fish, Jesus calms the waves, the great catch of fish, Paul's shipwreck.

Delightful Doorknobbers   25

An effective project for units on witnessing and evangelism, doorknobbers have wide application across grade levels. Suggested Bible stories and themes: Christmas, Baptism, evangelism, witnessing.

Accordion Book 9

Bible stories that include a progression of events are well suited to this project. Suggested Bible stories: creation, David and Jonathan, the ten plagues, Zacchaeus, Jesus stills the waves, the good Samaritan.

Candy Crèche 10

An ideal Christmas tie-in, this activity delights children of all ages. It makes a great project for special friends or for days when parents or grandparents are able to participate.

Glue Medallions 11

Easily adaptable to a wide range of Bible stories and themes, these medallions can be made by children of all ages and skill levels. Suggested Bible stories: Noah's ark, fishers of men, Jesus' death on the cross.

Praise Mobile 12

Conclude a hike or nature walk with this class activity. Suggested Bible concepts and themes: Psalm 136, praise verses, Thanksgiving.

"He Is Risen" Butterfly Mobile 13

This craft makes a festive Easter decoration for the Christian classroom. Because it can be adapted to a variety of themes, however, it can be used at any time throughout the school year. Suggested Bible stories and concepts: Easter, Jesus lives, creation, Baptism, Trinity.

Sparkle Rainbow 14

Although it takes a bit more time and skill, this craft results in a keepsake that will remind children that God kept His promise to save Noah and He keeps His promise to save us from our sins too. Suggested Bible stories: Noah's ark, God's promises.

Joy Maker 15

This craft is perfect for the enthusiasm young children have in singing their thanks and praise to their Lord and Savior. Suggested Bible stories and verses: Miriam's song, Mary's song, Psalm 57:1, Psalm 95, Psalm 96.

Clay Plaques 18

Celebrate Baptism birthdays and other festival days with this keepsake-quality craft idea. Encourage students to hang their plaque at home or to give it as a gift as a way to witness their faith in Jesus as their Savior from sin. Suggested Bible stories and themes: Christmas, Palm Sunday, Easter, Pentecost, Baptism.

Wooden Nativity 19

This craft project can be used as part of your Advent preparation. Students can make one item per week as they prepare their hearts and minds for the Messiah's birth. Suggested Bible stories and themes: Advent, Christmas, Epiphany.

Gospel in a Nutshell 20

John 3:16 is one of the first verses children learn. This craft project makes a unique Christmas gift or decoration for the classroom Christmas tree. It can be used to illustrate John 3:16, or any favorite Bible verse.

And the Seed Grew and Grew . . . 21

Children will be amazed to see God's creative power grow before their very eyes. Use this project in conjunction with science units. Suggested Bible stories and verses: parable of the sower, faith like a mustard seed, 1 Corinthians 3:6.

"I Ate Jonah" and Other Story Puzzles 22

To use this project with younger children, it's best to provide them with puzzle pieces you've already cut, then have children paint. Older children can design their own puzzle pieces. Suggested Bible stories: Jonah and the big fish, David and Goliath, Noah's ark, Christmas.

Rubber Stamp Set 23

Ink transfer is a neat and easy technique to incorporate into your art lessons. Combine this activity with a lesson on Christian symbols to extend learning. Suggested Bible stories, themes, and concepts: church year, liturgical symbols, God's love for us in the Person of Jesus Christ.

Swirling Paint and Paper 26

This craft can be a bit messy, so it's recommended for older students. It can be adapted for use with many Bible stories and can also be used in conjunction with science lessons. Suggested Bible stories and verses: Christmas, Jesus' Baptism, Easter, Holy Spirit, Pentecost, 1 Corinthians 13:12.

Paper-Bag Fish 27

In His public ministry on earth, Jesus often referred to fish. This quick and easy craft project is fun for all ages. Suggested Bible stories: Jonah and the big fish, fishers of men, coin in the fish's mouth, Jesus feeds 5,000, Jesus prepares breakfast for the disciples.

Watercolor and Ink Bible Story 28

This activity is easy to adapt for teaching almost any Bible story. Use it with students when bad weather keeps them indoors but they have lots of energy to expend. Suggested Bible stories: Moses and the burning bush, crossing the Red Sea, Daniel in the lions' den, Jesus heals the ten lepers.

Bookmark 29

Bookmarks are perfect for the first day of school or for those times when you need an activity on short notice. The added benefit is when students use their handmade bookmark, they grow in their understanding that God's Word is a gift to them. Suggested for any Bible verse, memory work, Baptism verse, or prayers.

"God's Gift to Me" Crest 30

Use this activity to teach children about the protection God provides through the power of His Word and Sacraments. Suggested Bible verses: Psalm 28:7, Ephesians 6:11–13.

MORE CONTENTS . . . .

Plaster Paperweights   31

For something a little different, these paperweights provide students with ample opportunity for creative expression. Suggested Bible stories and verses: Jesus is the rock/cornerstone, the parable of the builders, let your light shine, God's love for us.

Soda-Pop-Bottle Puppets   32
Tube Puppets   33
Stick Puppets   34
Box Puppets   35
Simple Puppets   36
Peanut Feet Puppets   37

Puppets are extremely effective as teaching tools. Combine these puppet activities with language arts by having students write plays based on Bible stories. Those featuring several characters are most appealing to children. Suggested Bible stories and themes: Queen Esther, Ruth and Naomi, Jacob and Esau, the ten plagues, Christmas, parable of the lost son, the good Samaritan, Zacchaeus, Maundy Thursday.

Pentecost Sculpture   38

The dramatic presence and creative potential of this craft makes it suited to boys and girls in third grade and beyond. Almost any small object or paper item can be used as ornaments. Suggested Bible stories and themes: Pentecost, Thanksgiving, Valentine's Day, spring.

Witness Windsock   39

All children, regardless of skill level, can easily, successfully, and quickly accomplish this activity. Suggested Bible stories and themes: Pentecost, witnessing.

Note or Recipe Cardholder   40

A great gift for Grandparent's Day, this craft results in an item that shares the Gospel message. Suggested Bible verses: Psalm 46:10, Psalm 62:1, Isaiah 25:1, Luke 11:28, 1 Corinthians 13:13, Philippians 4:13, Ephesians 4:32.

Rag Angel   44

Each student can make his or her own angel to hang on the classroom tree, and a large angel can be used as the tree topper. Suggested Bible stories and themes: the annunciation, the angel's announcement to the shepherds, various hymns.

Doily Dove   45

This craft is particularly striking when each child makes one (or more) and they are hung from the classroom ceiling. They can also be used as beautiful ornaments for a Christmas tree. Suggested Bible stories: Noah's ark, Holy Spirit, Pentecost, Jesus' Baptism, Christmas.

Block Puzzle   46

Older students who relish a more involved activity will enjoy this craft. Younger students can find it just as rewarding if the picture is already drawn on the blocks for them to paint. Suggested Bible stories: creation, Noah's ark, Jonah and the big fish, Christmas, Jesus' Baptism, Easter.

Foil Fun   47

An easy project for almost any age or skill level, this simple craft makes use of almost anything you have lying around at home or in the classroom. Suggested Bible stories: Easter, fishers of men, coin in the fish's mouth, Jesus feeds 5,000.

Heart Headband   48

This project calls for felt, but you could just as easily glue pre-cut foam shapes to a felt headband. Suggested Bible themes: Baptism birthday, Jesus' love for us, Valentine's Day, special friends, God's children.

Two by Two   49

This activity is ideal for Grandparent's Day or for Special Friend's Day (when older students are paired with younger students). Suggested Bible story: Noah's ark.

Puzzling Thoughts of God's Creation   53

This craft combines a variety of skills that makes it just right for kindergarten or first grade students. It's made almost entirely from recycled materials. Suggested Bible stories: creation, Noah's ark, Christmas, Easter, Jesus blesses the children, Jesus' miracles.

What's in the Egg?   54

Appropriate for science lessons, this activity helps teach children about God's creatures that hatch from eggs. Suggested Bible stories: creation, Easter.

Paper-Plate Puppet Stage   55

When you want to encourage students to tell Bible stories to others, have them make this simple storytelling prop. Suggested Bible stories: David and Jonathan, David and Goliath, Mary and Elizabeth, Jesus heals a blind man, Jesus forgives Peter.

Prayer Circle   56

This clever paper-cutting activity can be used as a memory verse or prayer aid for children who are comfortable using scissors. Suggested Bible stories: Jesus teaches us to pray, Jesus in the Garden of Gethsemane, Psalms.

Stand-Up Bible Story   57

This activity is best suited to teaching Bible stories that include a landscape or cityscape that creates a backdrop or tabletop stage. Suggested Bible stories: Adam and Eve sin, walls of Jericho, Solomon builds the temple, first Christmas night, Palm Sunday, the Last Supper, Jesus' crucifixion and resurrection.

Bottle of Waves   58

This is a fun, hands-on activity that children of all ages enjoy. Suggested Bible stories: creation, Jonah and the big fish, Jesus calms the waves, Paul's shipwreck.

"Joseph's Coat of Many Colors"
Paper Weaving   **41**

Made with readily available supplies, this activity promotes motor skill development. Use it to teach Christian symbols. Suggested Bible stories and concepts: Joseph's coat, baby Moses in the basket, God's love, the work of the Holy Spirit.

Talent Box   **42**

With unlimited options for decorating, this craft stimulates creativity. Suggested Bible stories and themes: widow's mite, the parable of the talents, serving, sharing, etc.

Theme Cross—Bible Story Review   **43**

To start the school year or wrap up with a review, this keepsake-quality craft is an engaging way to discuss faith basics and liturgical symbols. Suggested Bible concepts: Trinity, worship, church year, Good Friday, Easter.

Treasure Bag   **50**

You can readily adapt this project to fit the situation. Small bags can be used to illustrate Bible stories or as gift bags. Large bags can be used as book bags or to keep take-home papers neat. Suggested Bible stories: Wise Men, treasure in heaven, widow's mite, pieces of silver.

Noah's Animals in a Cage   **51**

This two-step craft is well suited to students who can manipulate scissors. Have them cut images from magazines first, then complete the activity. It can be adapted for almost any Bible theme. Suggested Bible stories: creation, Noah's ark, Christmas, Jesus feeds 5,000, Baptism.

Bug Box   **52**

For those times when students just can't stay indoors, plan to complete this craft first, then go on an insect collecting walk for a science unit. Suggested Bible stories and themes: creation, the ten plagues, Noah's ark, new life (spring).

"Jesus Feeds 5,000" Cut and Tell   **59**

This activity has maximum impact when you present it first to the class, then have the students pair off and practice it with one another. Suggested Bible stories: Jesus feeds 5,000, the great catch of fish.

Wallpaper 'Toons   **60**

When children are weary of drawing pictures, they can use wallpaper scraps to create two-dimensional Bible scenes. This craft is also effective using felt or printed scrapbooking sheets. Suggested Bible stories: God gives Moses the Ten Commandments, Abraham and Isaac, the good Samaritan, Philip and the Ethiopian.

Make a Mural   **61**

This activity requires that all students in the class participate. Learning occurs on several levels as children hear the Bible story, then work together to create a visual reminder. Use Sunday School leaflets to teach any Bible story.

Patterns   **62–64**

Craft Projects

Printed Banner

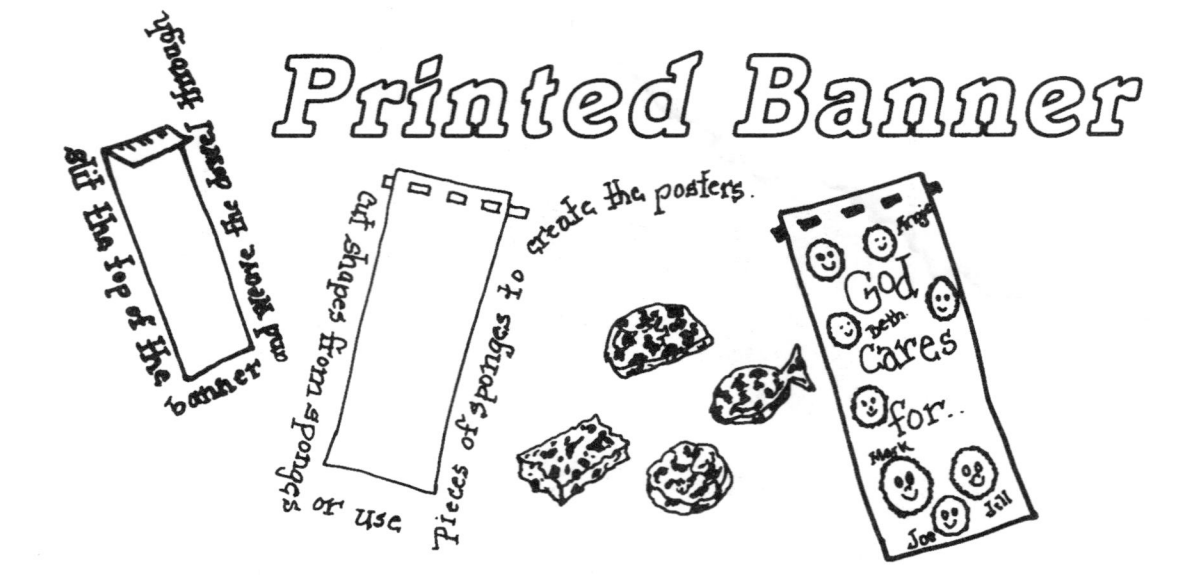

Whatcha Need

Old newspapers
Tightly woven material (burlap, felt, or vinyl)
Pinking shears
Dowel
Tempera paints
Liquid detergent
Marking pens
Paintbrushes
Sponges *
Yarn

Whatcha Do

1. Cover your work surface with old newspapers.
2. Cut the fabric banner background with pinking shears to the desired size. (9" x 18" makes a good sized individual banner.)
3. Turn over the top 2" of the banner. Cut slits into the fabric along the fold across the top.
4. Unfold the fabric and weave the dowel through the slits you just cut.
5. Mix 1 part detergent with 3 parts paint.
6. Use marking pens, paints, or letter-shaped sponges to print a Christian message on the banner.
7. Complete the banner, using sponges to paint designs.
8. Attach yarn to the ends of the dowel to hang the banner.
* Cut the sponges into the shapes you want or buy inexpensive shapes from a craft store.

Possible Themes:
Creation —"And It Was Good." (Use cookie cutters as patterns on the sponges.)
Noah's Ark—ark and rainbow. (Use pieces of sponge to paint ark and rainbow. Trace around animal cookie cutters on the sponges. Cut out shapes.)
"Gifts from God." (Cut sponges into shapes to represent gifts: love—heart; food—apple; everlasting life—butterfly; friends and/or family—circles with smiles; forgiveness—a cross.)

Window Shade Banner

Whatcha Need

- An old window shade
- Scissors
- Dowels (*optional*)
- Paints, marking pens, or fabric paints
- Yarn

Whatcha Do

❶ Use the whole shade to make one large class banner or cut it to make several smaller, individual banners.

❷ If you decide to use smaller pieces, fold the top over and put several slits in the fold.

❸ Unfold the shade and weave the dowel through the slits.

❹ Use paints, marking pens, or fabric paints to finish the banner.

❺ Attach yarn as a hanger.

Possible Theme:

"Unto Us a Child Is Born" (stable; Mary and Joseph; Baby Jesus; stars; shepherds; sheep)

Scripture Alphabet Banner

Matt 6:12

beZealous for the fear of the Lord Pr. 23:17

John 8:12

Mark 15:1

Mark 16:6

Matt 5:14

Matt 1:21

Whatcha Need

Tagboard
Scissors
A Bible
Fine-tipped marking pens
12' of ribbon at least 1/2" wide
Craft glue
Dowel

Whatcha Do

1. Have students cut 26 3" shapes from the tagboard.
2. Divide the class into equal groups, giving each group an equal number of alphabet letters to work with. Each group is to find one Bible passage that begins with those letters of the alphabet.
3. Write one Bible passage on each 3" shape.
4. Glue the shapes on strips of ribbon.
5. Turn the top of each piece of ribbon over the dowel and glue in place.

This activity is meant to be helpful in getting children into the Bible. Show them how to use a concordance to find Key words. As children look for verses encourage them to find verses that have a message for them.

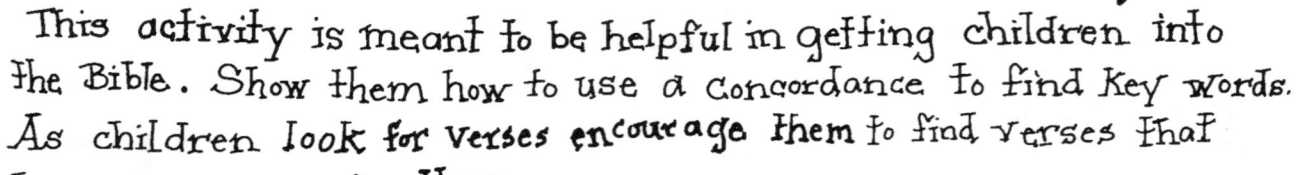

Accordion Book

Whatcha Need

7 pieces of tagboard, all the same size and shape
Marking pens and crayons
Sunday school leaflets and magazine pictures (optional)
Glue stick (optional)
Stickers, scrap paper, and other collage materials (optional)
Hole punch
Yarn or ribbon

Whatcha Do

1. Plan, write, and illustrate a favorite Bible story on the pieces of tagboard. Draw your own illustrations, or use pictures from Sunday school leaflets and magazines.
2. Create a cover using marking pens and stickers, scrap paper, or other collage materials.
3. Punch three holes in the sides of the pages and the cover and use yarn or ribbon to lace these together.
4. Share your books with each other and take turns retelling the Bible stories.

Note: You could use these and other Bible stories: the creation; the Good Samaritan; Zacchaeus; Christmas; Easter; David and Jonathan.

Encourage the children to write the Bible story in their own words!

9

Candy Crèche
Group Project

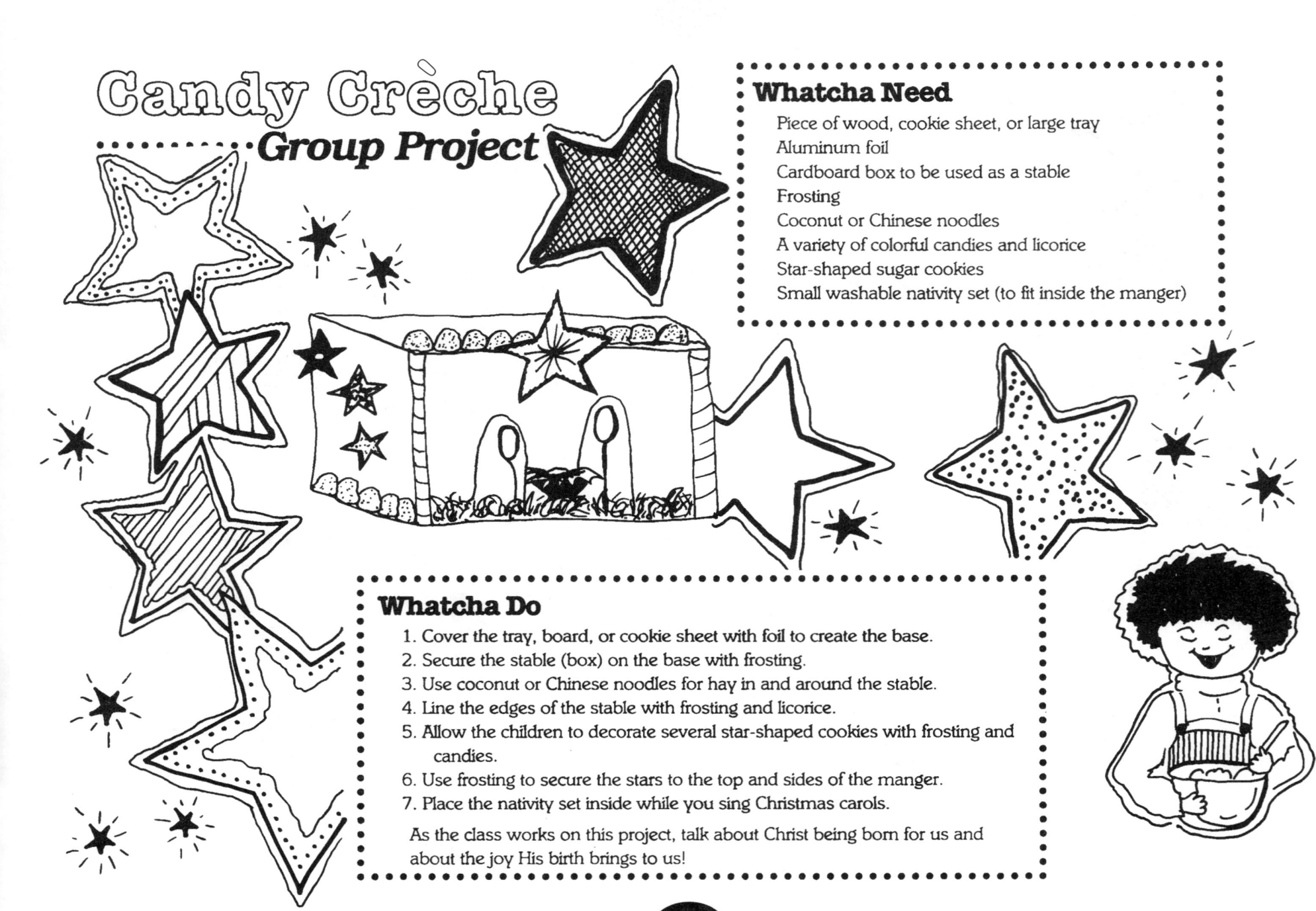

Whatcha Need

Piece of wood, cookie sheet, or large tray
Aluminum foil
Cardboard box to be used as a stable
Frosting
Coconut or Chinese noodles
A variety of colorful candies and licorice
Star-shaped sugar cookies
Small washable nativity set (to fit inside the manger)

Whatcha Do

1. Cover the tray, board, or cookie sheet with foil to create the base.
2. Secure the stable (box) on the base with frosting.
3. Use coconut or Chinese noodles for hay in and around the stable.
4. Line the edges of the stable with frosting and licorice.
5. Allow the children to decorate several star-shaped cookies with frosting and candies.
6. Use frosting to secure the stars to the top and sides of the manger.
7. Place the nativity set inside while you sing Christmas carols.

As the class works on this project, talk about Christ being born for us and about the joy His birth brings to us!

Glue Medallions

I am a fisher of men.

Whatcha Need

White glue
Food coloring
Cookie sheets
Waxed paper
Permanent marking pens
Hole punch
Yarn or shoestring

Jesus ♥ me!

Promise

Whatcha Do

1. Add a few drops of food coloring to the glue in the bottle to achieve a desired color.

2. Squeeze the glue from the bottle onto a cookie sheet covered with waxed paper. The children may make a blob or attempt to make a symbol. (Note: The table or desktop on which they work must be even and flat.)

3. Allow the glue to dry 24–48 hours, depending on the humidity in your area.

4. When it's completely dry, peel the glue from the waxed paper.

5. Decorate your medallion with colored marking pens.

6. Punch a hole in the top of the medallion and string yarn or a shoestring through it so you can wear it as a necklace.

7. Make a second medallion to give to a friend.

Note: Precolored glue may also be purchased.

Praise Mobile

Whatcha Need

A small tree branch

Items from nature (e.g., pinecones, nuts, seed pods, dried flowers, shells, drift wood)

Yarn or ribbon

A piece of tagboard decorated with the words "Praise God for His Creation" and a praise prayer.

Pictures of children (optional)

acrylic spray (optional)

Try seeds, nuts, shells, pine cones, leaves, drift-wood, feathers, sticks, stones...

Praise God for His creation for flowers & trees.
Praise God for His creation
Praise God for His creation for puppies & guppies.
Praise God for His creation for _ _ _ _ _ _
Praise God for His creation for _ _ _ _ _ _

Whatcha Do

1. Take a nature walk to collect items for the mobile, including a small tree branch.
2. Tie a piece of ribbon to each object you find.
3. Suspend the branch from the ceiling.
4. Tie nature items to the tree branch. You may also want to add pictures of the children. Remember that the secret of a mobile is to keep everything in balance!
5. Work together to write a praise prayer and write it on the tagboard. Attach the tagboard to your mobile.
6. Spray the mobile with acrylic spray. **(An adult should do this in a well-ventilated area away from the students.)**

The Praise Mobile will look different in different localities. Help the class as they write their praise litany. Use a phrase of response as an echo throughout the prayer. See **Psalm 136** as an example of this kind of responsive prayer or litany.

12

Whatcha Need

Butterfly patterns from p. 62 & 64

A sheet of acetate (e.g., the sheets sold for use with overhead projectors)

A variety of broad-tipped permanent marking pens

Scissors

Strip of tagboard or poster board, 2" x 18"

Stapler

A hole punch

Yarn or ribbon

"He Is Risen" Butterfly Mobile

Encourage the children to make their own designs.

Whatcha Do

1. Lay patterns for butterflies under the acetate.
2. Use a black marking pen to outline the butterflies. Work from top to bottom. (Do not touch the lines until they have dried, or they will smudge.)
3. After the lines have dried, cut out the butterflies.
4. Color the butterflies using permanent marking pens. Make each as colorful and bright as you can.
5. Print the message, "He Is Risen" on the strip of poster board and staple the ends together to form a circle. (Make sure students use the stapler with care; an adult should staple for younger children.)
6. Punch holes in the strip and use yarn to attach the butterflies to it. Add a hanger of yarn or ribbon at the top.

Variations: Use this process for any theme.

Family: "Jesus loves _____"

Put family members' names on hearts or drawings of the family.

Creation: "God made . . ."

Cut out pictures of the sun, moon, stars, flowers, animals, Adam and Eve.

13

Whatcha Need

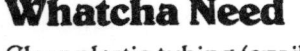

- Clear plastic tubing (available at craft, hardware, and aquarium supply stores), 1/2" in diameter
- Scissors
- Hot glue gun and glue
- Mineral oil or inexpensive baby oil
- Eye droppers
- Glitter in a variety of colors (at least four)
- Tagboard
- Clear fishing line
- Marking pens

Sparkle Rainbow

God always keeps His promises

Whatcha Do

1. Cut the tubing into four or five lengths. Note that each piece needs to be slightly larger than the last. Cut the first one, arc it, then arc the remaining tubing over it and cut it at the correct length for the second length of tubing, and so on. Cut as many arcs as you have colors of glitter.
2. Plug one end of each tube with glue from a hot glue gun. **(An adult should supervise this step closely!)**
3. Use an eye dropper to almost fill each tube with oil, one tube at a time. (Shake the tube gently as necessary to force out air bubbles.)
4. Add glitter and then more oil allowing for only one small air bubble in the tube.
5. Plug the second end of the tube with glue. Hold it upright until the glue dries. **(Again, adults must supervise use of the hot glue gun!)**
6. Repeat the process until you have filled and plugged all of the tubes.
7. Cut a piece of tagboard the length of your rainbow. The tagboard should be about 2" wide.
8. Glue the tubes onto the tagboard, creating the arcs of a rainbow.
9. When the glue dries, gently tie fishing line around the top of the rainbow as a hanger.
10. Print a Scripture verse or one of God's promises on the tagboard.

   Option: Use small, colored beads in place of the oil and glitter.

Joy Maker

Sing joyfully to the Lord

Rejoice in the Lord

Sing to the Lord a new song.

Whatcha Need

Contact paper, solid colored
Scissors
Plastic lid
Hole punch
Permanent marking pens
Jingle bells
Ribbon (curling ribbon works well)
Pipe cleaners (optional)
Stickers (optional)

Helpful Hint: Some bells have sharp edges and may cut through the ribbon. You may wish to use pipe cleaners to attach the bells. Then use ribbon to decorate the joy maker.

Whatcha Do

1. Cut the contact paper to fit the inside of the lid. Peel off the backing and carefully affix it to the lid.
2. Punch holes around the edges of the lid.
3. Using marking pens, write a message or Bible verse in the center of the lid.
4. Attach the jingle bells and, if necessary, extra ribbon to the holes.
5. Sing a song while making joyful sounds with your joy makers.

Witness Rocks

Whatcha Need

Rocks (clean and smooth)
Acrylic paint
Paintbrushes
Permanent marking pens

Glue a few rocks together.
Jesus my friend

Jesus is the rock.

Jesus ♥ me.

Make an extra rock for a friend or yourself.

This is the day the Lord has made. Ps. 118:24

Trust in the Lord with all your heart.

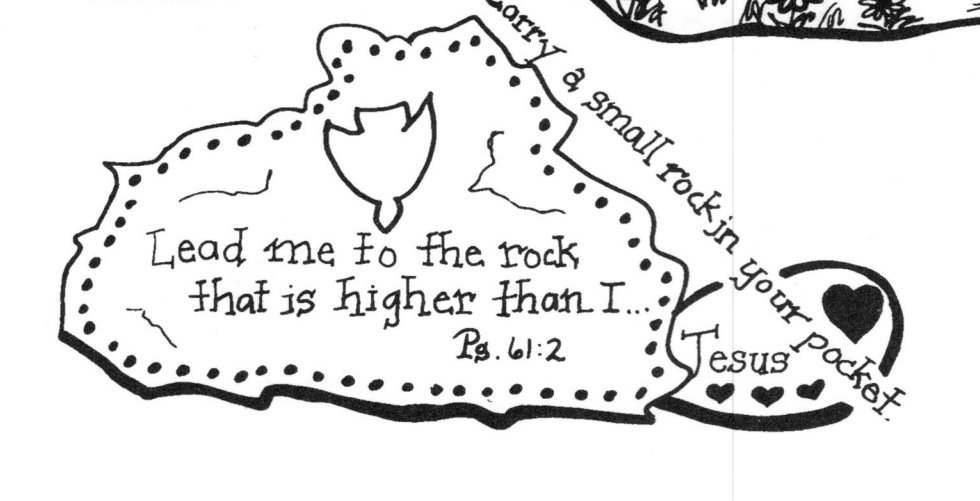

Carry a small rock in your pocket.

Lead me to the rock that is higher than I... Ps. 61:2

Jesus

Whatcha Do

1. The rock must be clean and very dry. Paint a Christian symbol on the rock. (**Caution: Acrylic paints are not washable; they will stain clothing. Wear paint shirts or old clothes as you work.**)
2. Use a permanent marking pen to put a Bible verse on the rock.
3. As you give away each rock you have made, explain the symbol or Bible verse you have used in your design.

   Children may wish to make several rocks—one to keep and several to give away.

Whatcha Need

- A shoebox lined with foil or plastic
- Sand to fill the box 3/4 full
- Spoon
- Rocks, buttons, sea shells, dried beans, costume jewelry (optional)
- Quick-setting plaster
- Paper clip

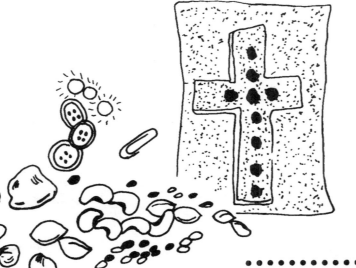

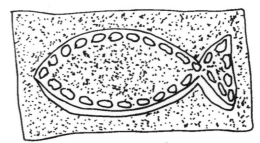

Jesus Christ, God's Son, Savior

Shoebox

Plaster of Paris

foil foil foil foil

sand

Spoon

Whatcha Do

1. Fill the box with damp sand approximately 4–5 inches deep.
2. Use a spoon or fingers to create a design in keeping with the theme of the lesson. The design should be approximately 2–3 inches deep. Add rocks, buttons, etc. if desired.
3. Mix the plaster according to directions on the package.
4. Pour the plaster into the box.
5. Hold the paper clip in place near the top of the figure until the plaster sets. This will make a hanger.
6. Allow the plaster to dry thoroughly.
7. Remove the plaster, brushing off the excess sand.

Sandcasting

Clay Plaques

Use with stories about creation - Baptism

- forgiveness - thanksgiving -

Whatcha Need

Self-hardening clay
22–32 gauge wire (approximately 2')
Waxed paper
Objects from nature (e.g., twigs, sticks,
    leaves, nuts, shells, rocks, evergreen sprigs)
Rolling pin
Pencil
Shoe polish (liquid or paste)
Soft cloth
Clear spray shellac or acrylic

Whatcha Do

1. Use wire to slice off a slab of clay, approximately 1/2" thick.
2. Place the clay on waxed paper.
3. Arrange objects from nature on the clay.
4. Place another sheet of waxed paper over the arrangement.
5. Roll a rolling pin over the waxed paper to press the objects into the clay.
6. Remove the waxed paper and the objects.
7. Use a pencil to drill a hole at the top of the clay slab.
8. Allow the clay to dry according to directions on the package.
9. Use shoe polish to color the plaque. Buff with a soft cloth. Work carefully so the clay doesn't break.
10. Spray the plaque with clear shellac or acrylic. **(An adult should do this in a well-ventilated area away from the children.)**

Whatcha Need

Wooden blocks cut from 1" x 2" pieces of wood *

Sandpaper

Fine-tipped permanent marking pen, (e.g., Sharpie)

Acrylic or craft paint

Paintbrushes

Shellac or clear acrylic spray

* Make animals 3" long; people, 6" long; the manger, 4" long (note that you will turn the manger sideways). To make 4 people, 2 sheep, and a manger, you will need a board 34" long.

Whatcha Do

1. Sand the ends of the wood blocks.
2. Draw an outline of Joseph, Mary, and two shepherds, each on a 6" block.
3. Draw an outline of a sheep on each 3" block.
4. Turn the 4" block on its side and draw a manger on it.
5. Paint each figure.
6. Outline each figure with a fine paintbrush or black permanent fine-line marking pen.
7. Shellac or spray with a clear acrylic. **(An adult should do this outside, away from the children.)**

The figures should be kept very simple.

Children may wish to design each figure on paper first.

Gospel in a Nutshell

Whatcha Need

A whole walnut
Paint (optional)
Glue
Ribbon
Fine-tipped permanent marking pen
Quilling paper

Whatcha Do

1. Paint the nut (optional).
2. Place glue along the "seam" of the walnut.
3. Press ribbon along the glue. Join ribbon ends at the top and make a loop for a hanger.
4. Use a permanent marking pen to write **John 3:16** on one side of the nut and your name on the other.
5. Write the words "For God so loved . . ." on a strip of quilling paper and glue it at the top where the ribbon meets. Place the end of the paper at the joint so it looks as if it's coming out of the walnut.

Variation: To make a Christmas ornament, paint the nut white, green, or red, and add a ribbon of the same color. Hang the decorated walnuts on dresser knobs, bedposts, or on peg shelves.
Make several of these and give them away to share the Gospel.

And the Seed Grew

Whatcha Need

A natural sponge
Water
A variety of fast-sprouting seeds (lima beans, peas, etc.)
2 ribbons

Whatcha Do

1. Wet the sponge; squeeze out excess water. (Water should not be dripping from the sponge.)
2. Fill the holes in the sponge with seeds.
3. Tie one ribbon around the sponge, placing a bow on top. Knot the bow.
4. Attach the second ribbon to form a loop.
5. Hang the sponge in a window and watch the seeds grow.
6. Keep the sponge moist.

Use this project anytime you teach about the power of God's Word or when you study the parable of the sower. Remind older students that God often tells us that His Word is like seed—powerful and life-giving, even though we cannot always see its power.

21

"I Ate Jonah" and Other Fun Story Puzzles

Jonah
big fish - a man - a heart

Whatcha Need

Plywood, 8" x 12" (one piece per child)
Pencils
Sandpaper
Paint (three different colors, tempera or acrylic; if you use tempera, add a small amount of white glue to the paint)

Use the puzzles to tell and retell the Bible Stories.

Whatcha Do

1. Give the children an 8" x 12" piece of plywood and a pencil. Ask them to design a jigsaw puzzle based on the Bible story you are studying. Tell them that thin pieces may break while cutting, so they should try to draw simple pictures with thick pieces. No puzzle should have more than four pieces. As they design their puzzles, tell them that each piece should be contained in the next larger piece, so bigger pieces of the puzzle "eat up" the little pieces while you retell the story.

2. **After the children have drawn their design on the board, have an adult use a jigsaw to cut out the pieces.**

3. Sand and paint the puzzle pieces.

Younger children can paint the puzzle pieces and retell the story. Older children can design their own pieces and then paint them once the puzzle is cut out.

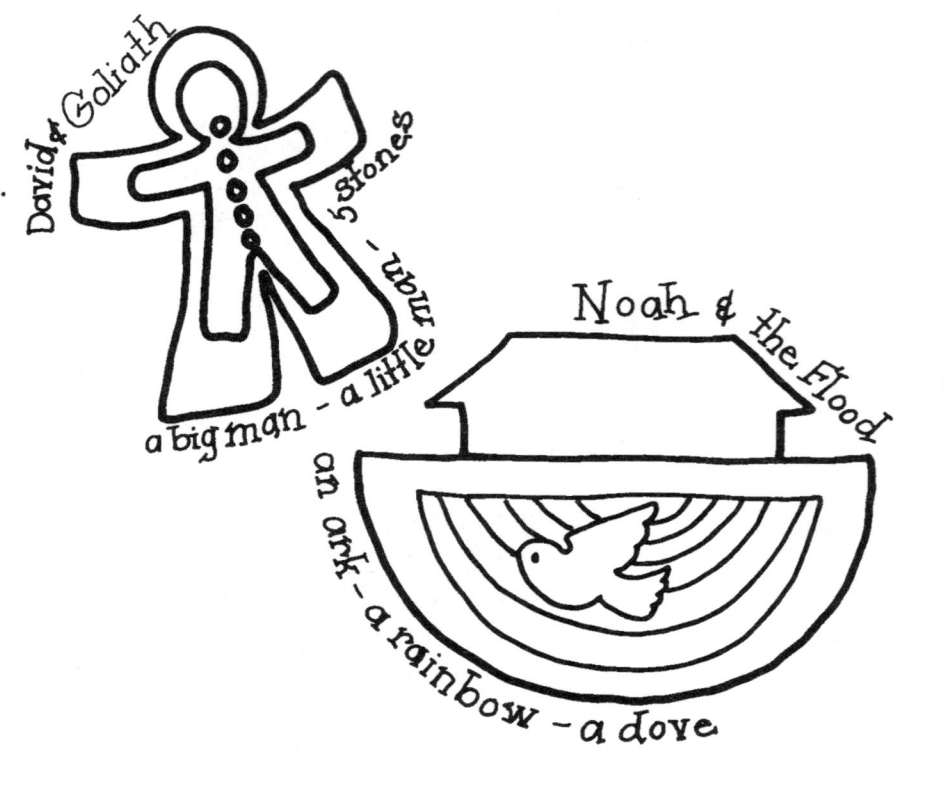

David & Goliath
5 stones
a big man - a little man

Noah & the Flood
an ark - a rainbow - a dove

Rubber Stamp Set

wood. foil . . . . . If you do not have an old inner tube – glue yarn on a wood block, making your favorite design.

Whatcha Need

Inner tube from a truck tire

Scissors

Empty spools or scraps of
    two-by-fours, each 3"–4" long.

Rubber cement

Ink pads or paint

Print on paper. boxes . bags . cards . bookcovers

Paint

Ink Pad

Cards

Inner Tube

boxes

bags

Rubber Cement

yarn

Whatcha Do

1. Cut shapes, letters, numbers, or words from the piece of inner tube.
2. Glue these to the boards or spools with rubber cement. (Remember that letters, words, and numbers must be glued on backward to print correctly. Look at your design in a mirror before you cut it out!)
3. Use paint or ink to print.

Noah's Ark

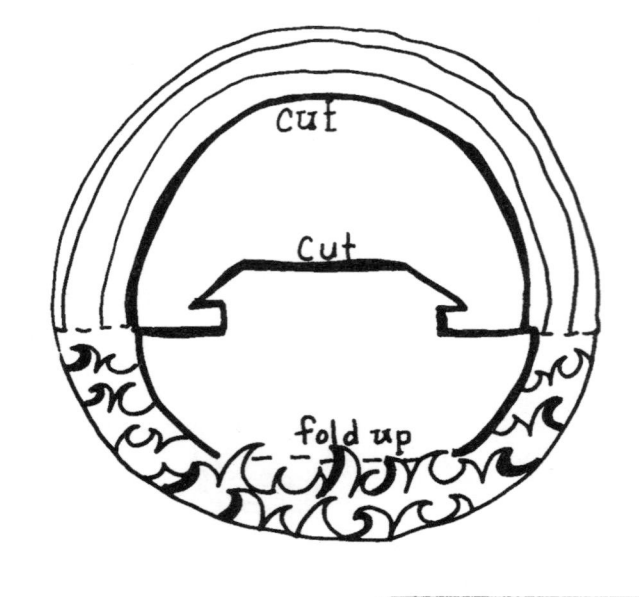

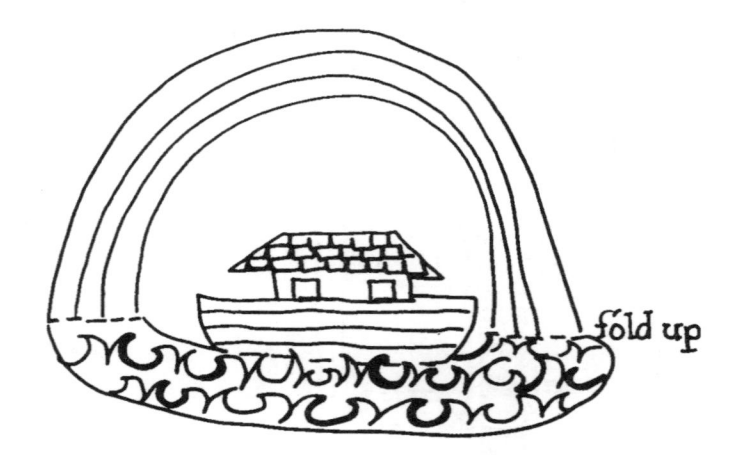

Whatcha Need

An 8" paper plate, white
Marking pens or crayons
Scissors
Animal crackers
Glue

Whatcha Do

1. Draw a pattern on the paper plate as shown in diagram 1.
2. Color the rainbow, water, and ark.
3. Cut along the lines as shown.
4. Glue animal crackers to the ark.
5. Fold the ark and the rainbow up at the base of each to create a 3-D effect.

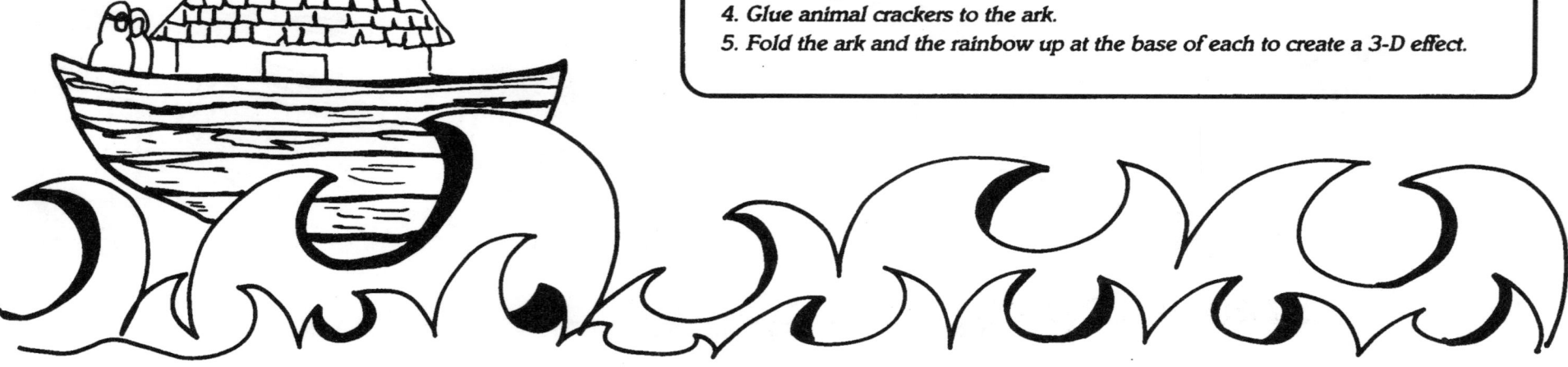

Delightful Doorknobbers

Whatcha Need

Construction paper in a variety of colors,
   2 sheets per doorknobber
   (one 4-1/2" x 12"; one 4" x 11")
Pencil
Scissors
Glue
Marking pens
Glitter, rickrack, sequins, buttons, jingle
   bells (*optional*)

Whatcha Do

1. Fold the smallest sheet of construction paper in half.
2. Draw one or two symmetrical shapes along the fold (hearts, crosses, crowns, flames, flowers, Christmas trees, butterflies, etc.). Be sure to leave room at the top for the doorknob hole.
3. Cut out the shapes.
4. Unfold the paper and glue it to a larger piece of a contrasting color.
5. Cut a hole near the top for the doorknob.
6. Decorate with marking pens and other materials.
7. Add a message or Bible verse from the lesson.

Note: These make cheery "get well" cards—something a little different in a hospital room. It's also a great way to share a message with neighbors, or just as a reminder of God's great love for us.

Swirling Paint and Paper

Use more than one color.

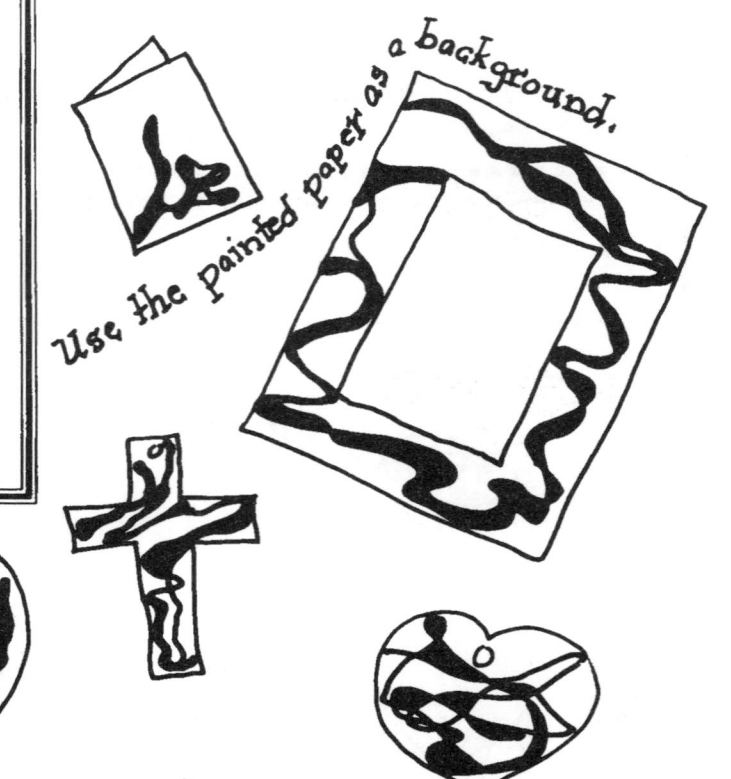

Use the painted paper as a background.

Use paper or light weight

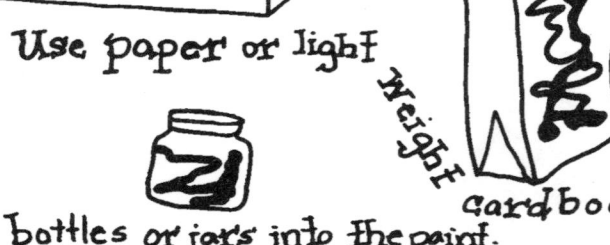

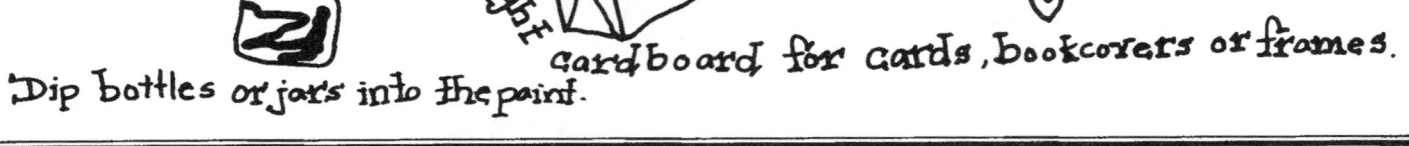

cardboard for cards, bookcovers or frames.

Dip bottles or jars into the paint.

Whatcha Do

1. Fill the foil pan with 2–3" of water.
2. Use the toothpick to add small drops of paint to the water and swirl it. (Use one or two colors of paint.)
3. Gently lay a sheet of paper on top of the water, then lift the paper from the water with a tweezers or tongs.
4. Carefully shake off the excess water and set the paper aside to dry.
5. When the paper has dried, use it for cutouts, frames, or greeting cards. Decorate it with Bible verses, Christian symbols, or other witnessing messages.

Paper-Bag Fish

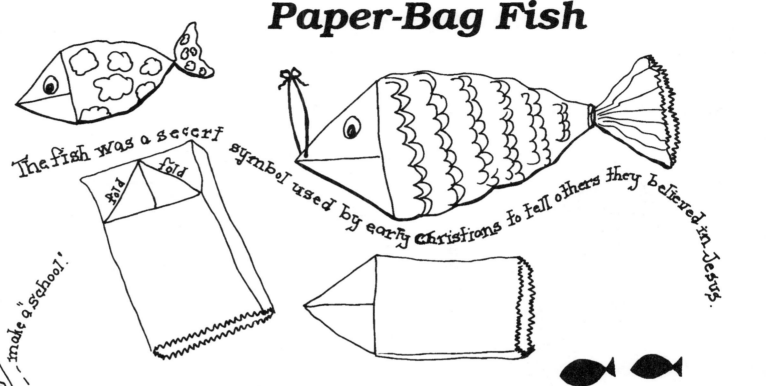

The fish was a secret symbol used by early Christians to tell others they believed in Jesus.

"make a school!"

Make many more fish!

IXOYE

Whatcha Do

1. Use paint, marking pens, and/or construction paper to decorate both sides of the bag.
2. Fold the bottom corners in, as shown, to make the head of the fish.
3. Use crumpled newspaper to stuff the bag about half full.
4. Use the rubber band to secure the top third of the bag to create the tail.
5. Punch a hole in the top and attach a loop of yarn to make a hanger.

Watercolor and Ink Bible Story

Whatcha Do

1. Place a piece of paper in water, then pull it out. Let the water drip off for a few seconds.
2. Lay the paper on a pad of old newspapers.
3. Using a paintbrush, drop and lightly brush paints of different colors onto the wet paper. The colors will blend together.
4. When the paint is thoroughly dry, use a dark marking pen to draw the Bible story on the background sheet you just made.
5. Frame the painting.

28

Bookmark

Whatcha Need

Watercolor paper, 2" x 7" strip
Marking pens
Clear contact paper or access to a laminating machine
Scissors
Hole punch
A narrow ribbon

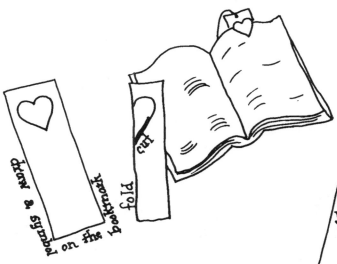

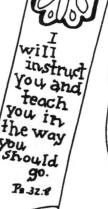

Whatcha Do

1. About 1" from the top of the paper, draw a simple Christian symbol (anchor, cross, butterfly) and color it with a marking pen.
2. Decorate the rest of the bookmark. Write an appropriate Bible passage on the bookmark.
3. Cover both sides of the bookmark with clear contact paper or laminate it.
4. Fold the bookmark in half lengthwise (but do not crease it) so you can cut along the outline of the bottom half of the symbol you colored in. (See the illustration.)
5. Punch a hole in the top of the bookmark.
6. Tie a ribbon (or two ribbons) through the hole.

29

"God's Gifts to Me" Crest

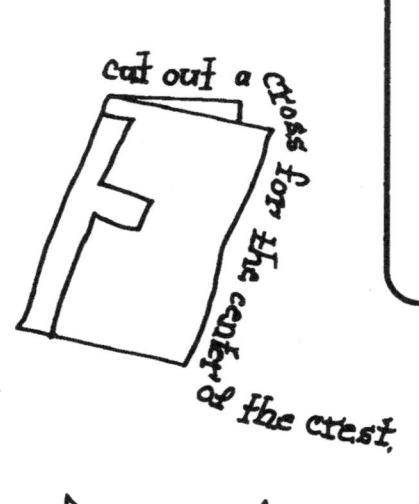

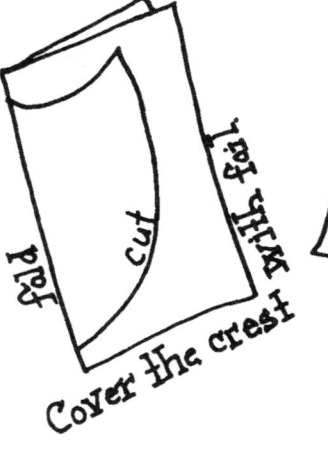

cut out a cross for the center of the crest.

cover the crest with foil

fold   cut

back the crest with foil

Whatcha Need

Poster board
Scissors
Aluminum foil
Glue
Construction paper
Photograph of each child
Colored marking pens or crayons
Ribbon

God's gifts to me!

Plaster Paperweights

Pour mixture into a bag – leave the bag open – squeeze and hold.

Let your light shine.

Jesus is the Rock

Whatcha Need

Plaster of paris
Water and bowl
Sturdy plastic bags
Sandpaper
Paint or marking pens
Shellac or spray acrylic (optional)
Felt
Scissors
Glue

Whatcha Do

1. Mix plaster according to directions for a quick set.
2. Pour it into bags and squeeze it to create an interesting shape. (Do not twist-tie the bag; simply hold it closed.)
3. Hold the plaster in place until it begins to harden.
4. When it has set, remove it from the bag.
5. Use sandpaper to smooth any rough edges.
6. Use paints or marking pens to decorate it.
7. Spray your sculpture with acrylic spray or shellac. (An adult should do this in a well-ventilated area away from the students.)
8. Cut a piece of felt to fit the bottom of the sculpture. Glue it in place.

Soda-Pop-Bottle Puppets

–children –friends –teachers–

–a Samaritan –disciples–

Kings –shepherds– –Joseph –Mary–

Whatcha Do

1. Turn the bottle upside-down.
2. Use collage materials to decorate it. For hair, use 30 strands of yarn,
    12"–18" long. Tie the shank of yarn in the center. Glue it to the
    bottom (now top) of the bottle. To make arms, use cones or rolls of
    paper. Glue these to the sides of the bottle.
3. Insert the dowel into the bottle as shown and tape it in place.

32

Tube Puppets

Set up a table of collage materials and encourage the children to create their own Bible characters. Use the puppets to tell and retell the Bible stories.

Whatcha Need

Paper towel tubes
Miscellaneous items to decorate puppets
   (e.g., buttons, ribbons, cotton balls)
Construction paper, wallpaper,
   or fabric scraps
Glue
Brown or white strips of paper approxi-
   mately 3" x 4"
Marking pens
Yarn

Use cotton balls to make sheep.

Try foil for the King's crown.

Whatcha Do

1. Use construction paper, wallpaper, fabric scraps, and other collage materials to decorate the paper towel tubes.
2. Use a strip of brown or white paper at the top of the tube to make the puppet's face. Add the facial features with a marking pen.
3. Glue yarn to the top for hair.

Stick Puppets

Whatcha Do

1. Cut paper or tagboard to the approximate size you want the puppets to be.
2. Use marking pens and collage material to create puppets to tell today's Bible story or to make real-life applications of Biblical truths.
3. Cut out the puppets and glue them to paint-stirrer sticks or to tongue depressors.

Ask the children to make the characters from the Bible stories. Use the puppets to tell the story.

Box Puppets

Whatcha Need

Small raisin boxes or gelatin boxes
Scissors
Construction paper or aluminum foil
Glue
Miscellaneous items to decorate puppets (e.g., buttons, yarn, puff paints, colored glue)
Craft sticks

Encourage the children to create their own characters.

Whatcha Do

1. Cut the top flaps off the boxes.
2. Cover the boxes with construction paper or foil. (Have younger children simply cover the front and back; leave the sides and bottom as they are.)
3. Use yarn, buttons, colored glue, paints, and whatever other glorious junk you can find to make faces on the boxes.
4. Glue the craft stick to the inside of the box or place the open part of the box on your fingers and use the box as a finger puppet.

Note: Gelatin boxes work well with the craft sticks. Raisin boxes are small enough for use with fingers.

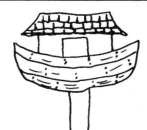

folded to make them stand.

Keep the puppets slightly

fold

fold

Shepherd   King

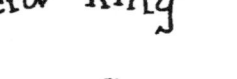

fold

fold

manger

fold

angel

fold

lamb

Simple Puppets

Encourage children to use their imagination in dressing the puppets.

Whatcha Do

1. Use the patterns on p.63 to make the puppet figures. Fold your heavy paper in half, trace the pattern and cut out the figure.
2. Open the figure and decorate it to make a puppet character. The fold will allow the puppets to stand.
3. Encourage the children to create their own patterns for additional puppets.

   Young children love to act out stories using puppets, especially puppets they have made. Older children's puppets will become more detailed.

   You may use these puppets to tell or review Bible stories, or to act out life-related applications of Bible truths.

Peanut Feet Puppet

Whatcha do

1. Fold the paper in half.
2. Draw a 6" tall Bible character on one side.
3. Cut out the picture, using the folded paper so that you will have two identical characters.
4. Color in the features and clothes of your Bible character.
5. Glue the bodies together with the toothpicks coming out of the bottom as legs.
6. Stick the toothpicks into the marshmallow peanut candies, using the candies as the character's feet. Stand.

Pentecost Sculpture

Pull apart and twist.

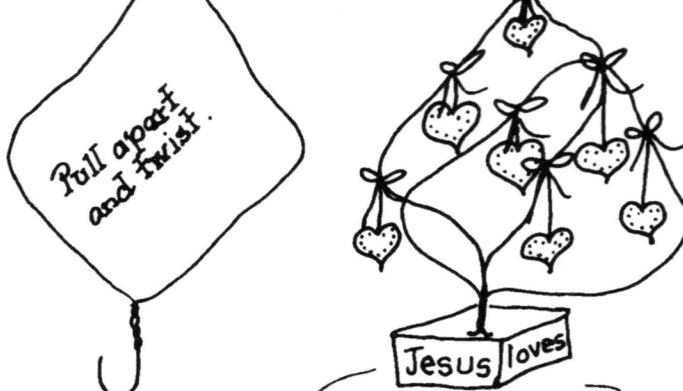

Jesus loves

Whatcha Need

Two wire coat hangers
Plaster of paris
Bottom half of a half-gallon milk carton
Cardboard or wooden dove and flames
Paint or marking pens
Foil *(optional)*
String or yarn

God's Children

Whatcha Do

1. Bend the hangers into interesting shapes. To do this, pull each hanger into a diamond shape then twist it slightly.
2. Mix plaster of paris according to directions and pour it into the milk carton. Secure the hangers in the plaster, holding them in place until set.
3. Decorate the dove and flames with paints or marking pens, or cover them with foil.
4. Remove the milk carton from plaster. Decorate the plaster base using marking pens or paint. Write a Bible passage around the base.
5. Hang the dove and flames from the hangers.

Variations: New life theme (butterflies); Christmas symbols; *"God cares for my family"* symbols

38

Witness Windsock

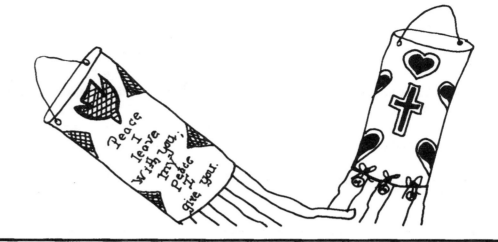

Whatcha Need

A piece of construction paper,
12" x 18"

Scissors

Foil, cellophane, or contrasting
colors of construction paper,
12" x 18"

Glue or glue stick

Tape

Marking pens

Contact paper or access to a
laminating machine

Florist, plastic, or foil ribbon

Stapler

Hole punch

Yarn

Jingle bells

Whatcha Do

1. Fold the piece of construction paper into fourths, vertically.
2. On the fold lines, draw symbols that tell people you are a Christian (hearts, fish, cross, butterfly, etc.). Be sure to discuss the meaning of each symbol with the class.
3. Carefully cut out the shapes. Then open the paper and glue pieces of foil, cellophane, or construction paper to the back of the open spaces you just made to create silhouettes of the symbols on the windsock.
4. Put a piece of tape all the way across the top and all the way across the bottom edges along the back side of the wind sock. This will reinforce the holes you will make in steps 9 and 10.
5. Use marking pens to decorate the front side of the windsock. Use an important biblical truth or a Bible verse that relates to the lesson.
6. Cover both sides of the windsock with contact paper or laminate it. This will allow the windsock to hang outside as a witness to all for a long time.
7. Staple, tape, or glue 8–11 ribbons along the bottom, inside edge.
8. Roll the windsock into a cylinder and staple or tape in place. (Supervise older students carefully. Do not let younger children use the stapler themselves.)
9. Punch two holes at the top edge of the windsock and attach yarn as a hanger.
10. Punch holes along the bottom edge of the windsock and tie on the jingle bells.

Hang the windsock outside to tell all who come to visit that Jesus lives in your home.

Note or Recipe Cardholder

Whatcha Need

Clip clothespin
Craft or acrylic paint
Paintbrush (very small)
Small tiles (from a tile store)
Ribbon (very narrow)
Glue
Magnet strip

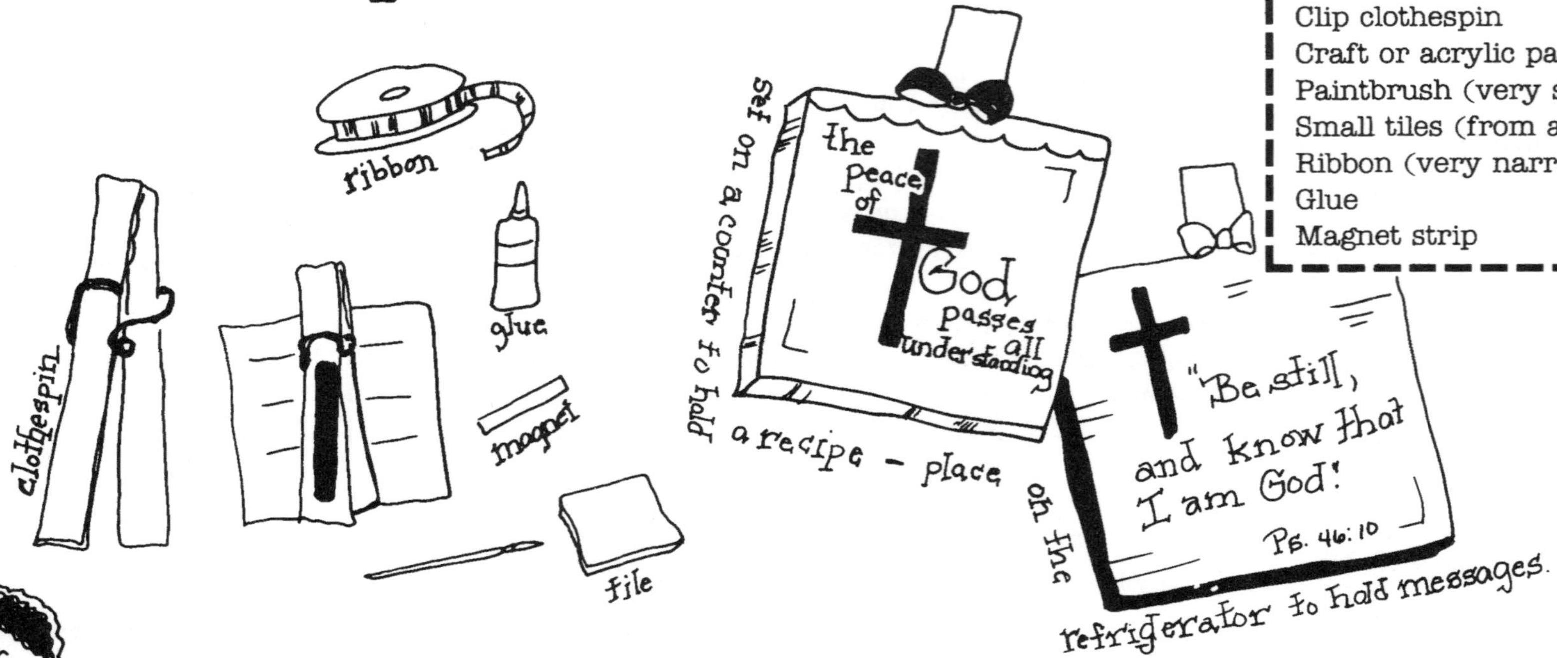

ribbon

clothespin

glue

magnet

file

The peace of God, passes all understanding

"Be still, and know that I am God!" Ps. 46:10

set on a counter to hold a recipe — place on the refrigerator to hold messages.

Whatcha Do

1. Paint the clip clothespin.
2. Use the paint to decorate the tile.
3. Glue the ribbon around the outside edge of the tile.
4. Glue the clothespin to the back of the tile. The clip end needs to be at the top as shown in the illustration.
5. Glue a magnet strip to the back of the clothespin. Make sure the magnet strip is strong enough to hold the clothespin and tile securely to a metal surface.

When it's completed, use the project to hold messages on the refrigerator or set it up on a counter to hold recipes.

"Joseph's Coat of Many Colors"

 cut various shapes from construction paper. weave contrasting colors through the shapes.

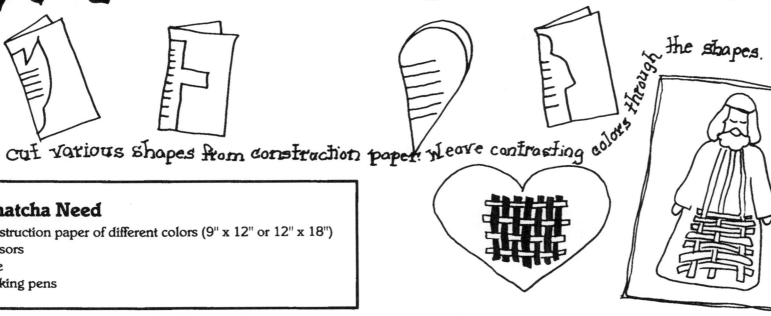

Whatcha Need

Construction paper of different colors (9" x 12" or 12" x 18")
Scissors
Glue
Marking pens

Whatcha Do

1. Let each child choose a variety of pleasing colors of construction paper.
2. For the background, draw Joseph's coat on a piece of construction paper.
3. Cut approximately six vertical lines in the mid-section of the coat. (If you like, you can also cut four thinner lines into each sleeve.)
4. Cut several strips of paper, approximately 1" wide and in a color that contrasts with your "coat." (If you've decided to work with sleeves, use 1/2" strips for this.)
5. Weave the strips in and out, securing each end with glue. Trim off any excess.
6. When you have woven all the strips, use a marking pen to outline the coat. Add other details too.

Note: Young children will find larger paper easier to handle.

Variations: Adapt this project to any Bible story subject. Or use it as you work with simple Christian symbols.

Talent Box

Whatcha Need

One medium-size box (cereal box, shoebox, etc.)
Gift-wrapping paper
Cellophane tape
Ribbon or bow
Crayons or marking pens
Paper
Scissors
Glue

I can help.
I can serve.
I can sing.

a good friend

Prayer

My Talents
are Gifts
from God.

Help the children identify the many talents and gifts God gives them.

Gifts from God.   I can help.

Thank You, God
For voices
   that sing
      praises.
Thank You, God.
For hands
   that serve
      people.
Thank you, God
For _____
   That _____
   _____
Thank You, God.

Whatcha Do

1. Wrap the box as a gift.
2. Discuss the talents God has given us. Ask the children to draw pictures of their talents on paper.
3. Cut out the pictures and glue them to the boxes.
4. Help the children to write a prayer of thanks.
5. Glue the prayer to the box.
6. Give your box a title, such as "My Talents Are a Gift from God."

Theme Cross—
Bible Story Review

Whatcha Need
Seven plain tiles, each 3" square (found at a local tile store)
Acrylic paints
Paintbrush
One 12" wood slat
One 21" wood slat
Wood glue
A self-adhesive picture hanger

Whatcha Do

1. Paint a picture on each tile to depict a different Bible story (e.g., several Christmas narratives, the Passion/Easter accounts, stories you've studied lately in VBS or Sunday school). If necessary, fill in with Christian symbols so that each of the seven tiles is painted.
   (Note: Acrylic paint will not wash out of clothing. Wear old clothes or ask all students to wear paint shirts.)
2. Glue the short wood slat to the longer slat about 6" from one end to make a cross.
3. Glue each tile you painted onto the wooden slats.
4. Attach the picture hanger to the back of the cross near the top.

Whatcha Need

Muslin, torn into 10 strips, each 1" x 4-1/2"; and 13 strips, each 1" x 13"
1" Styrofoam ball
Narrow ribbon cut in 3 pieces, each 8" long
Glue gun
Silver or gold pipe cleaner

Rag Angel

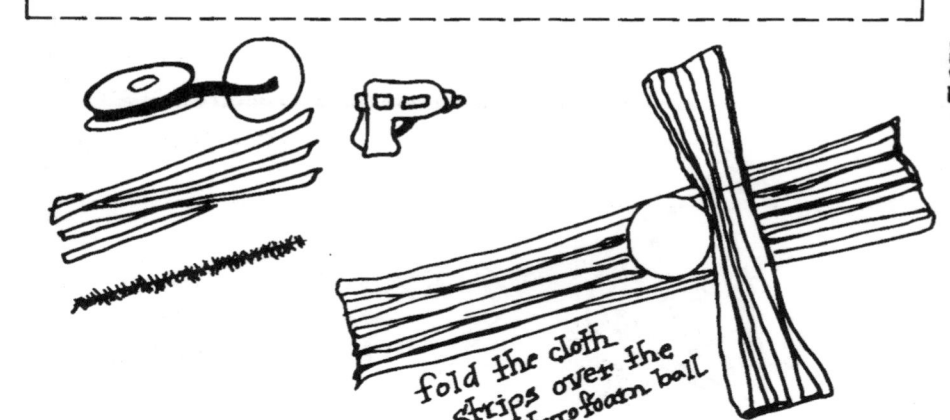

fold the cloth strips over the Styrofoam ball

Whatcha Do

1. Lay the long strips of muslin down side-by-side.
2. On top of these strips, about 5" from one end, lay the 4-1/2" strips perpendicular to the longer strips.
3. Place the Styrofoam ball (the angel's head) directly below the 4-1/2" strips.
4. Gently bring the ends of the 13" strips over the Styrofoam ball to make the angel's head. Make sure the ball is completely covered.
5. Use a piece of ribbon to tie these strips in place directly beneath the head and above the 4-1/2" strips, which have become the arms. Tie a knot, then a bow. Be sure to tie these strips tightly.
6. Tie a piece of ribbon directly beneath the arms. Tie a knot, then a bow.
7. Tie the third piece of ribbon in a knot to make a loop. Attach it to the back of the angel with a hot glue gun. **(An adult should use the hot glue gun.)**
8. Use half of the pipe cleaner (about 3") to form a halo. Glue the halo to the top of the angel's head.

Doily Dove

Whatcha need

Dove pattern
White poster board
Scissors
One 10" white lace doily

One 8" white lace doily
Tape
Hole punch
Yarn or string

yarn

tape

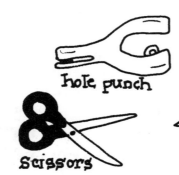

hole punch

Scissors

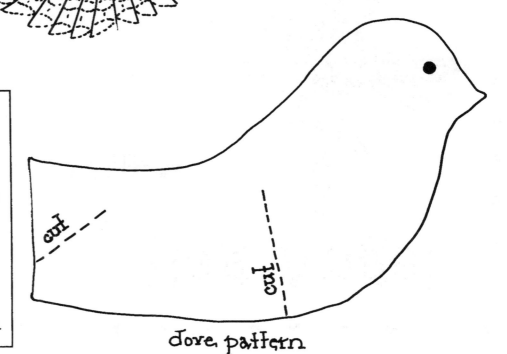

dove pattern

cut

cut

Whatcha do

1. Trace the dove pattern onto the poster board.
2. Cut out the dove.
3. Cut the two slits into the dove as shown in the diagram.
4. Accordion-fold the 10" doily and slide the middle of the doily into the front slit, making the wings.
5. Accordion-fold the 8" doily and slide the middle of the doily into the back slit, making the tail.
6. Tape each doily lightly into place.
7. Hang the dove from the ceiling or light fixture.

Note: Christians use the dove as a symbol for peace and the Holy Spirit.

45

Whatcha need

- Four blocks of wood, 2" x 3" x 2"
- Sandpaper
- Plain paper, 8" x 12"
- String or yarn
- Tempera paint
- Paintbrush
- Brown shoe polish (paste, not liquid)
- Soft cloth
- Clear acrylic spray
- **Note: This project could be nicely framed.**

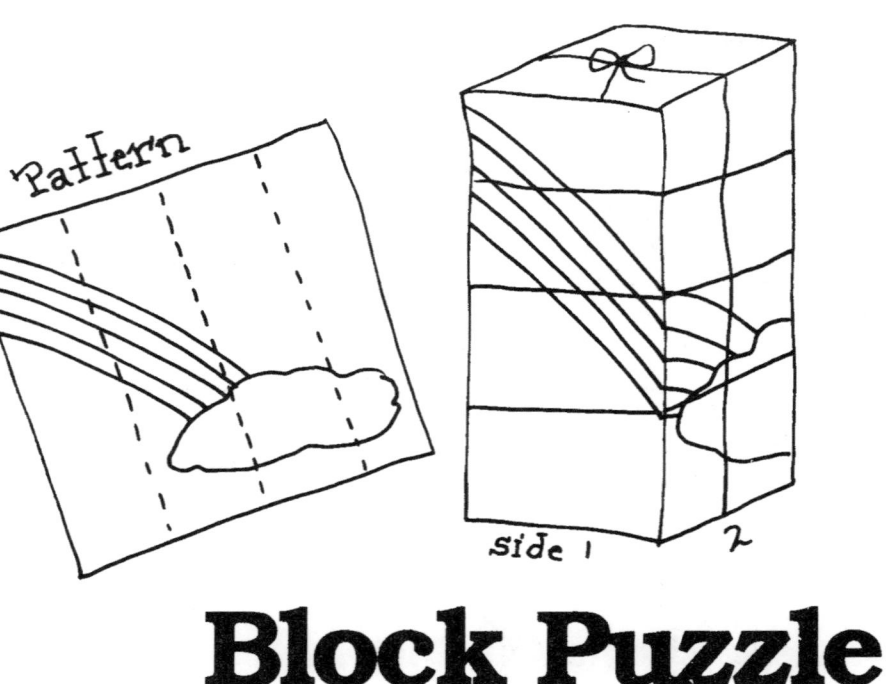

Block Puzzle

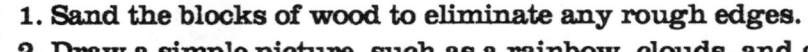

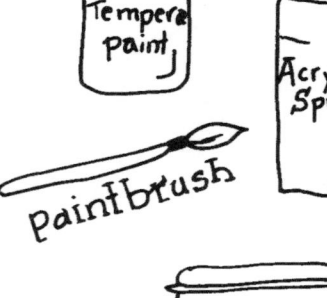

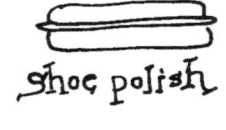

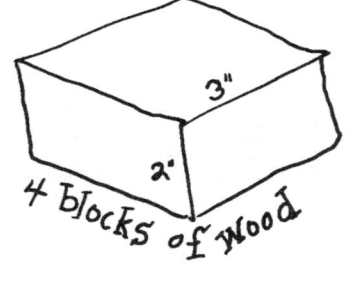

Whatcha do

1. Sand the blocks of wood to eliminate any rough edges.
2. Draw a simple picture, such as a rainbow, clouds, and grass on the plain paper.
3. Fold the picture in half and in half again, so that when it is opened, it will be divided into four equal parts vertically. Each quarter section will be painted onto a side of the four blocks.
4. Place the four blocks on top of each other and tie with a string or yarn to keep them together.
5. Lay the blocks down and draw ¼ of the picture on each side of the blocks.
6. Paint the picture onto the wooden blocks, removing the string from sides 1 and 3 after sides 2 and 4 have been painted. When dry, tie the string going up and around sides 2 and 4 to paint sides 1 and 3. Let dry.
7. Remove the string completely and discard.
8. Use a soft cloth to lightly rub brown shoe polish over all sides of the cubes to give them a stained look.
9. Spray with acrylic spray. **(An adult should do this in an area away from children.)**

Foil Fun

© 1993 Concordia Publishing House

Whatcha need

Junk (nails, paper clips, tokens, bolts, sticks,
    pencil stubs, bottle caps)
Heavy cardboard
Glue
Aluminum foil
Shoe polish (paste, not liquid)
Soft cloth

Whatcha do

1. Collect small junk items.
2. Glue the items to a piece of heavy cardboard in the desired shape.
3. Tear a piece of foil 2" larger than the cardboard.
4. Gently press the foil over your junk sculpture to fit the form, being careful
   not to tear the foil.
5. Glue the foil to the back of the cardboard to keep it in place.
6. Rub shoe polish, using a soft cloth, over the foil to give it an antiqued
   look.

Note: This project looks good with a slat frame around it.

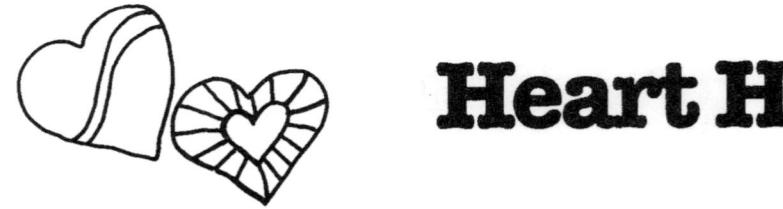

Heart Headband

cut out

fold

cut out area

fold

fold

fold

Decorate your headband with craft paints, beads, sequins - - - - - - - -

Whatcha do

1. Cut two 2" x 12" strips of felt.
2. Fold one of the strips like a fan three times.
3. Trace the heart pattern on this page onto the first folded section. Cut the pattern, remembering not to cut through the folded ends.
4. Repeat steps 2 and 3 with the second strip of felt.
5. To connect the two strips to wear as a headband, cut the end of each strip as shown and hook the ends together.

Note: For smaller heads, you may have to cut off a heart at one end and then make the cuts to hook them together.

This project can also be done with crosses.

Whatcha need

Felt

Scissors

Two by Two

animal crackers

pin back

glue gun

Acrylic Spray

Whatcha need

Two animal crackers
Craft paint (optional)
Glue gun
Clear acrylic spray
Pin backs

Whatcha do

1. Paint the animals crackers with craft paint.
2. Glue the two like animals together, one following the other. Let dry.
3. Spray with acrylic spray. **(An adult should do this outdoors in a well ventilated area, away from children.)** Let dry.
4. Glue on the pin backs. **(An adult should use the glue gun.)**

Variation: Paint the animals with brightly colored fingernail polish.

Whatcha need

Pinking shears
Fabric
Fabric paints or puff paints
Glue gun
Needle
Embroidery thread

Treasure Bag

Whatcha do

1. Use the pinking shears to cut the fabric into a 4" x 12" rectangle.
2. On the top half of the rectangle, paint a decoration or symbol. Let dry.
3. Fold the bottom half back and use a glue gun to attach the sides, front to back. **(Have an adult use the glue gun.)**
4. Thread the needle with 4 strands of embroidery thread.
5. Stitch around the top of the bag, starting at the front, 1" from the top; leave 3" to 4" of thread at each end.
6. Tie a knot in each end of the thread to keep if from pulling through.
7. Place your goodies in the bag and use the thread as a drawstring. Tie a bow to close your package.

Noah's Animals in a Cage

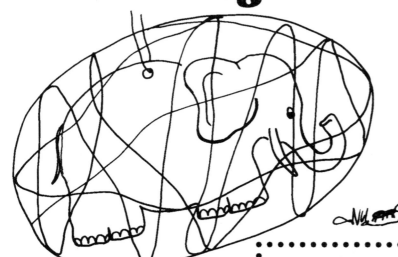

Whatcha need

Balloon
String or yarn
White glue
Hole punch
Pictures of animals (from magazines or made by the children)

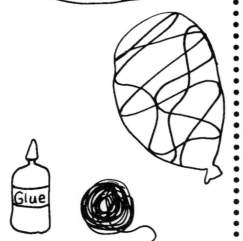

Whatcha do

1. Blow up the balloon.
2. Dip the string or yarn into white glue; wrap it around the balloon many times until it resembles a cage. Let dry overnight.
3. Pop the balloon and remove its pieces from the cage. **(For safety to children and animals, be sure to throw away *all* pieces of the balloon.)**
4. Punch a hole at the top of the animal; hang it by a string from the top inside of the cage.
5. Tie a string at the top of the cage to hang it.
6. Hang all the animal cages in one area for your "zoo" of animals.

Bug Box

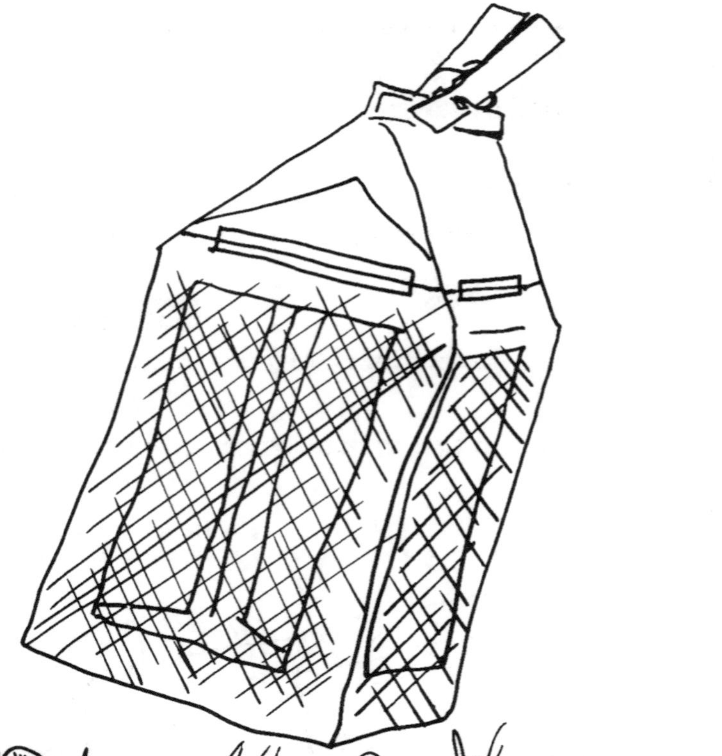

Whatcha need

Half gallon or quart milk carton
Scissors
Old nylon pantyhose
Tape
Clothespins

Whatcha do

1. Cut out all four sides of the milk carton, leaving the corners intact.
2. Cut the legs off a pair of old pantyhose. Pull a leg up from the bottom of the milk carton; tape it just above the "windows."
3. Leave the top open to put in God's small creatures.
4. Close the top with clothespins. Observe.
5. Leave the small creature in the box only long enough to enjoy and watch. Let the creature(s) out at the end of class so they can go back to nature to do the jobs God gave them to do.

Whatcha need

Four empty juice boxes

Plain wrapping paper or tissue paper

Tape

Scissors

Full page magazine pictures (from zoo newsletters, *National Geographic*, *Your Big Backyard* magazines)

Glue

Clear contact paper (*optional*)

Puzzling Thoughts of God's Creation

cut

magazine

wrapping paper

Tape

Glue

Juice boxes

Whatcha do

1. Wrap each juice box with wrapping paper or several layers of tissue paper, as if you're wrapping a present.
2. Carefully cut out a full-page picture from a nature magazine.
3. Fold the picture in half, and in half again.
4. Cut it into four equal pieces.
5. Glue the picture onto the sides of the four juice boxes to make a puzzle. (You could double your fun and make it more challenging by doing both sides of the boxes with another picture.)
6. You might want to put clear contact paper over the picture to protect the puzzle, or tape the edges.

What's in the Egg?

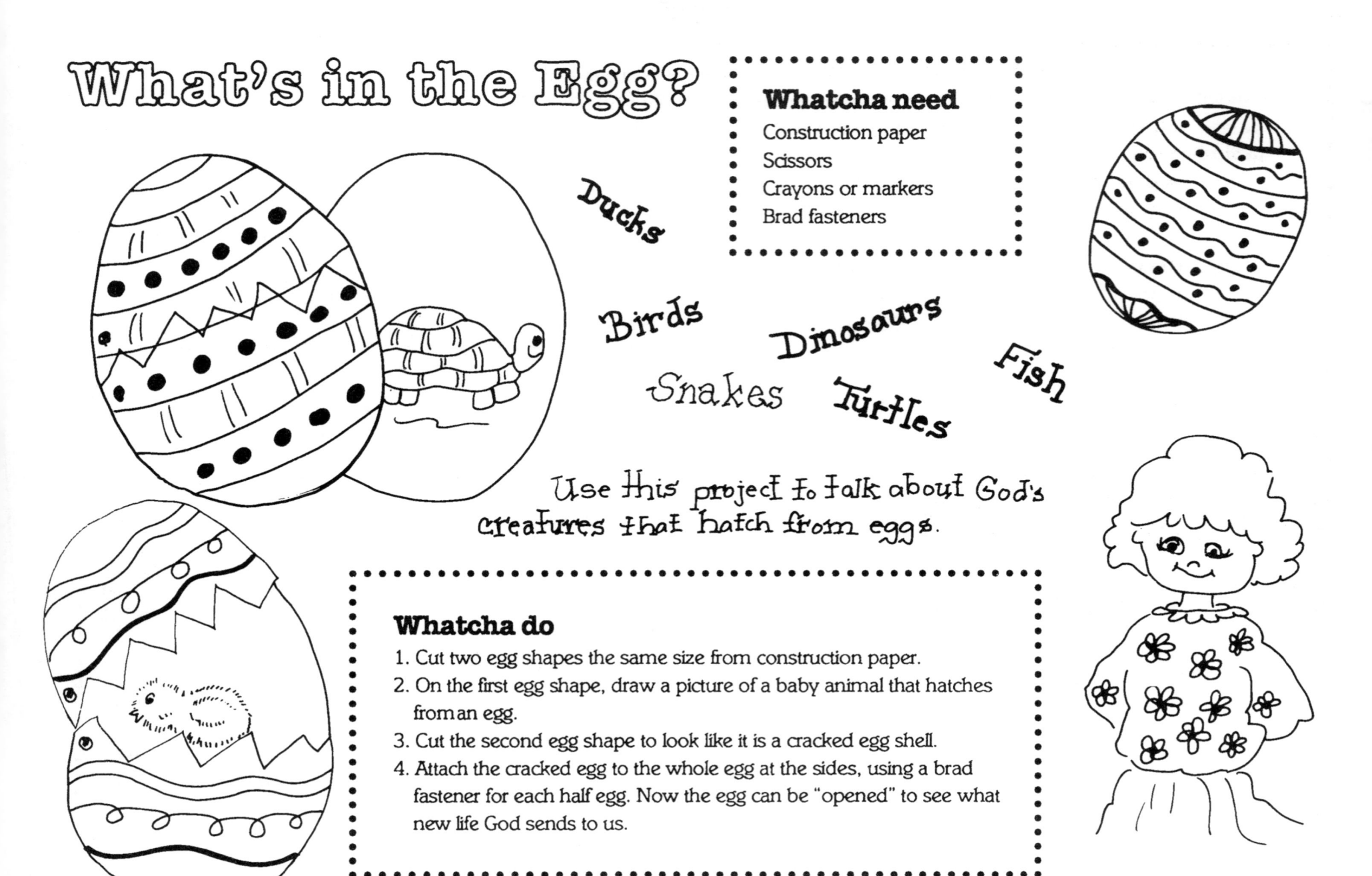

Ducks

Birds

Dinosaurs

Fish

Snakes

Turtles

Use this project to talk about God's creatures that hatch from eggs.

Whatcha do
1. Cut two egg shapes the same size from construction paper.
2. On the first egg shape, draw a picture of a baby animal that hatches from an egg.
3. Cut the second egg shape to look like it is a cracked egg shell.
4. Attach the cracked egg to the whole egg at the sides, using a brad fastener for each half egg. Now the egg can be "opened" to see what new life God sends to us.

Paper-Plate Puppet Stage

Whatcha need

- One 8" paper plate
- Fine-line markers
- Scissors
- Craft sticks

Whatcha do

1. Decorate the bottom half of the paper plate to be the ground (draw rocks, bushes, roads or paths).
2. Decorate the top half of the paper plate to be the sky (draw clouds and blue sky).
3. Cut a slit across the middle of the plate (about 4½—5" across) to separate the land and sky. You will insert each puppet through this slit from the back.
4. To make the puppets, draw a face and clothes on the top of the craft sticks. Leave room at the bottom of the sticks to hold the puppets.

Note: You may want to make two or three each of male and female puppets. These can be adapted to whatever Bible story is being presented.

Each child now has his or her own cast of characters and a puppet stage to tell a favorite Bible story to a friend or family member.

Prayer Circle

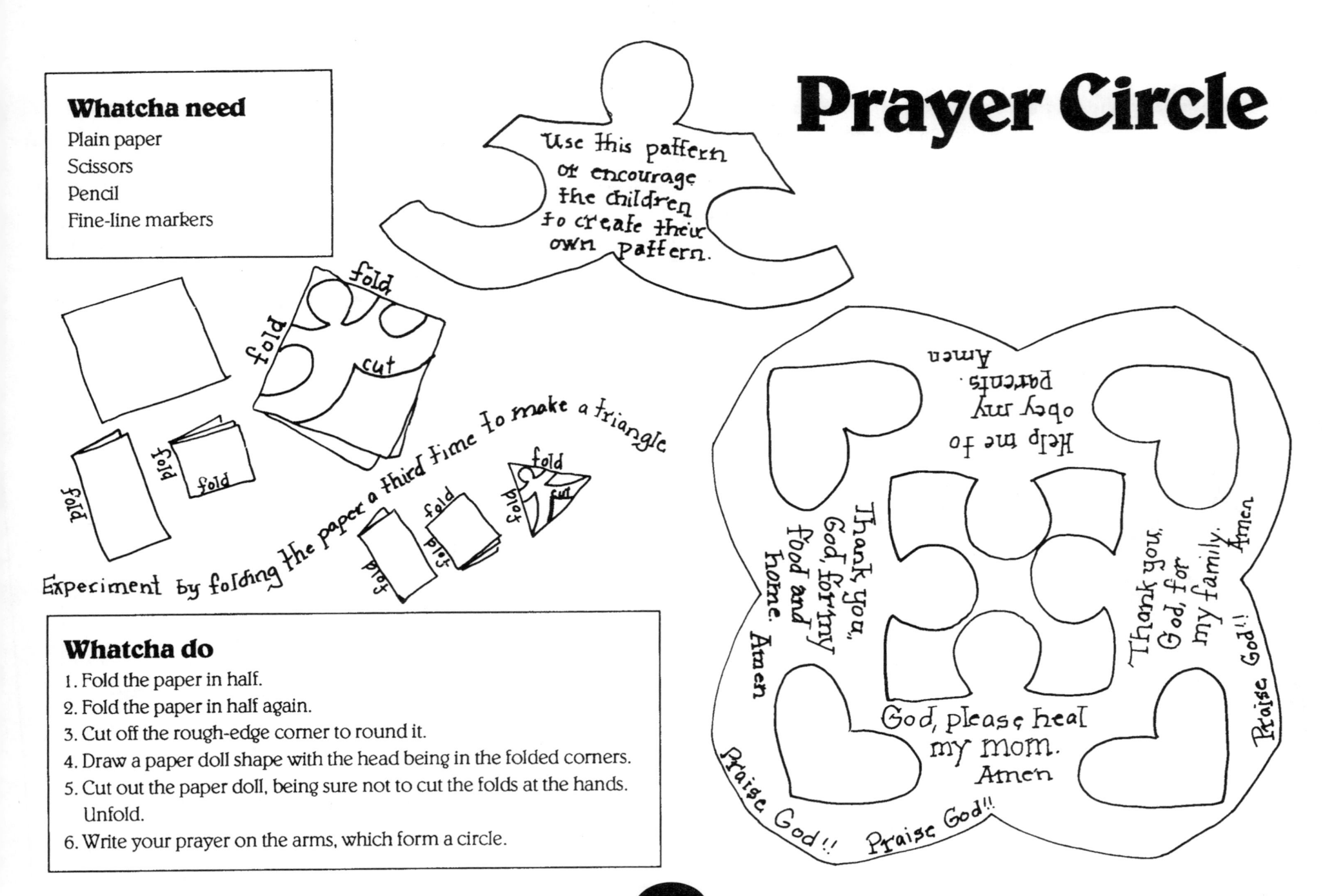

Whatcha need

Plain paper

Scissors

Pencil

Fine-line markers

fold

fold

cut

fold

fold

fold

Experiment by folding the paper a third time to make a triangle

fold

fold

fold

cut

Use this pattern or encourage the children to create their own pattern.

Whatcha do

1. Fold the paper in half.
2. Fold the paper in half again.
3. Cut off the rough-edge corner to round it.
4. Draw a paper doll shape with the head being in the folded corners.
5. Cut out the paper doll, being sure not to cut the folds at the hands. Unfold.
6. Write your prayer on the arms, which form a circle.

Help me to obey my parents. Amen

Thank you, God, for my food and home. Amen

Thank you, God, for my family. Amen

God, please heal my mom. Amen

Praise God!!

Praise God!!

Praise God!!

Stand-Up Bible Story

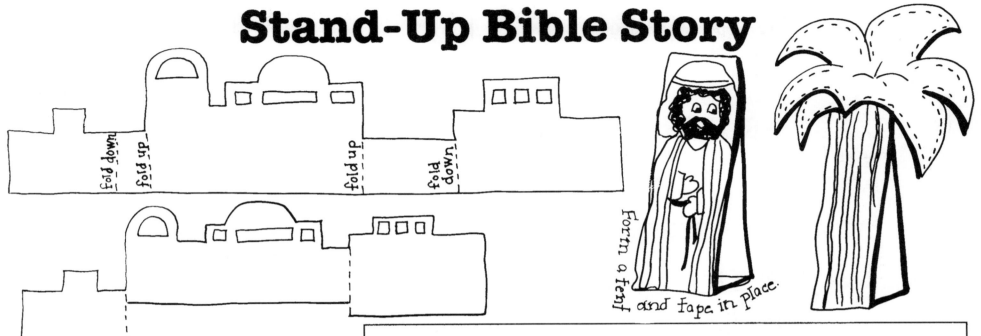

form a tent and tape in place.

Whatcha do

1. Draw a Biblical city skyline on a piece of construction paper about 18" x 6".
2. Cut out the skyline.
3. Fold according to the diagram. The skyline will then be two-dimensional and it will stand up.
4. To make puppets, cut strips of construction paper for each character in the Bible story (approximately 1" x 10").
5. Fold each strip in half. About $\frac{1}{2}$" to $\frac{3}{4}$" from the bottom, fold again to form the base.
6. Draw Bible characters' faces and clothing on the folded strips of paper, using both the front and the back.
7. Refold the bottom to form a tent shape. Tape in place.

Note: Use the puppets and the city scene to tell or retell a Bible story. For "Jesus Feeds 5,000" use a landscape that includes trees and bushes.

Whatcha need

Construction paper
Pencil
Scissors
Markers
Tape
Fabric scraps *(optional)*

Bottle of Waves

Remove the base.

Glue the caps on the bottles.

waves

oil

water

Water

Add shavings of crayons to water.

Crayon

Crayon

blue food coloring

Whatcha do

1. Remove the bottom cover from the plastic 2-liter bottle.
2. Fill the bottle 3/4 full of water. Add several drops of blue food coloring, then fill to the top with oil. Pour the oil into the water slowly.
3. Close tightly.
4. Hold the bottle horizontally and tip the bottle from side to side.

Variation: Fill the bottle ⅞ full of water. Add crayon shavings and close tightly. Turn the bottle upside down and watch the colors "dance."

Whatcha need

One plastic 2-liter soda bottle
Water
Cooking oil or mineral oil
Blue food coloring
Crayon shavings (optional)

"Jesus Feeds 5,000" Cut and Tell

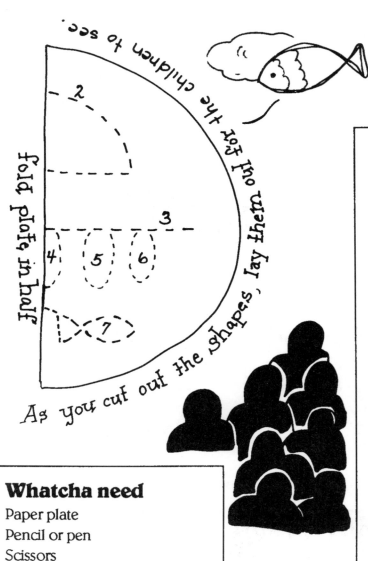

fold plate in half

As you cut out the shapes, lay them out for the children to see.

Whatcha do

Before class, draw lines onto a folded paper plate as shown in the diagram.

As you tell the Bible story, fold and cut as indicated by the numbers given in the story example. (This activity needs to be practiced before class.)

1. **Jesus and His disciples went for a boat ride to a quiet place.**
2. **When people found out where Jesus was, they went to see Him on the mountainside.**

   (Hold up the plate as you cut out #2 as the mountain.)

   Many people wanted Jesus to heal them.
3. **As evening came, the disciples began to worry about how all of these people would have something to eat.**
4. **Jesus told the disciples to feed the people.**
5. **The disciples told Jesus that they could find only five fish and two loaves of bread.**
6. **Jesus told the disciples to bring the food to Him. He gave thanks to God and broke the bread.**
7. **The disciples passed food out to all the people there that day. There were 5,000 people who ate the fish and bread!**
8. **When everyone was filled with food, the disciples picked up 12 baskets of food that were left over!**

Whatcha need

Paper plate

Pencil or pen

Scissors

Wallpaper 'Toons

The Good Samaritan

The Robbers

The Priest

The Levite

The Samaritan

The Inn

Whatcha need

Wallpaper books
Scissors
Glue
Tape

Glue

Scissors

Tape

Wallpaper books

Whatcha do

1. As a group, choose a Bible story.
2. Choose four to five scenes from the story. Children may work on each page as individuals or in groups of two or three.
3. Choose the appropriate number of wallpaper pages to be the background of each scene.
4. Cut shapes out of the wallpaper to make the scenes (homes, trees, roads, people).
5. Glue the shapes onto the background paper.
6. Have a representative from each group tell what is happening in their scene.
7. The scenes can be taped together or put on a bulletin board to tell the story in correct sequence.

Make a Mural

Butcher paper works

Well for the mural.

Whatcha need

Plain paper (three times the size of the Bible story picture), one piece per child

Bible story pictures (from Sunday school or vacation Bible school lesson leaflets)

Scissors

Glue or tape

Crayons or markers

Whatcha do

1. Cut the Bible story picture into four or five vertical sections (one section for each child in your class).
2. Cut the plain paper into the same number of strips.
3. Give each child one section of the Bible story picture and one strip of white paper.
4. Each student will use crayons or markers to reproduce their section of the Bible story picture onto the strip of white paper.
5. When all students have completed their pictures, glue or tape their sections together to form the mural. (You might want to tape the original Bible story picture together and hang it beside their mural to see the comparison and contrast.)

Encourage children to make their own patterns or if they use these patterns---

---encourage individuality

The star led the wisemen to the Christ child.

a shepherd's staff

The Holy Spirit

and creativity

The fish is a secret symbol used by early Christians to tell others they believed in Christ.

The butterfly represents New Life and reminds us of Christ's resurrection.

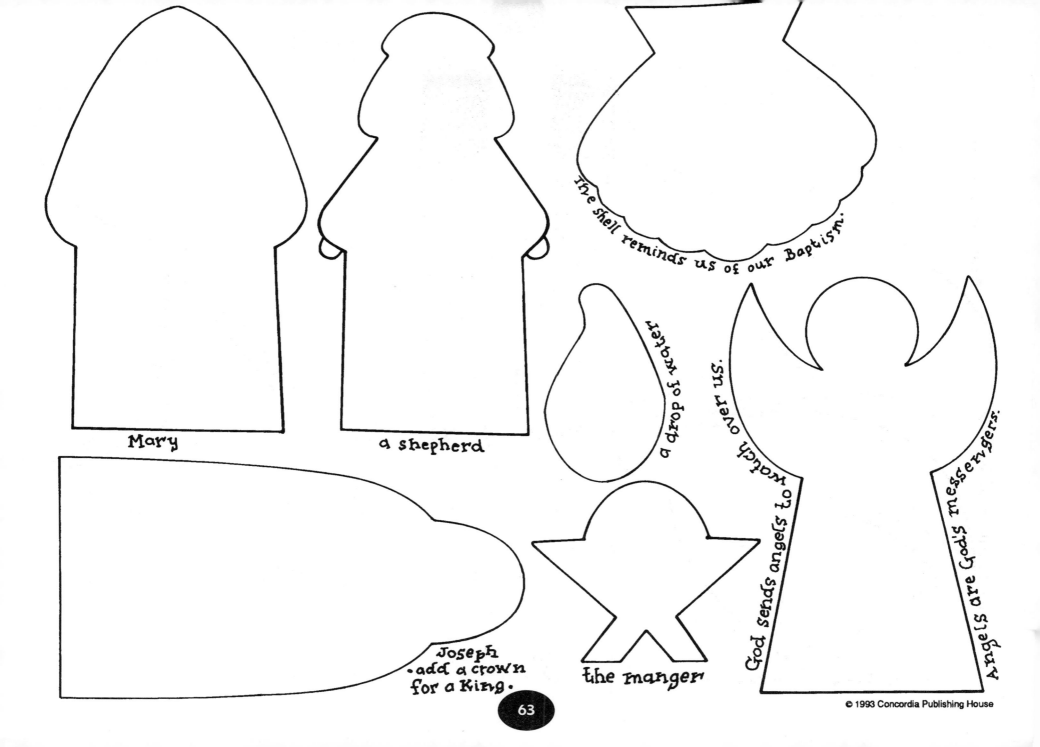

Mary

a shepherd

The shell reminds us of our Baptism.

a drop of water

Joseph
•add a crown
for a King.

the manger

God sends angels to watch over us.

Angels are God's messengers.

63

The ☧ is made up of the first two Greek letters of the word Christ.

New Life

Christ is our anchor.

Christ the King